HAL•LEONARD

INSTRUMENTAL
PLAY-ALONG

FLUTE

 AUDIO ACCESS INCLUDED

PLAYBACK+
Speed • Pitch • Balance • Loop

A NEW MUSICAL

WICKED

TITLE	PAGE
As Long as You're Mine	2
Dancing Through Life	4
Defying Gravity	6
For Good	8
I Couldn't Be Happier	10
I'm Not That Girl	11
No Good Deed	12
No One Mourns the Wicked	24
One Short Day	14
Popular	16
What Is This Feeling?	18
The Wizard and I	20
Wonderful	22

T0082057

To access audio visit:
www.halleonard.com/mylibrary
Enter Code
6380-7182-5766-0511

ISBN: 978-1-4234-4966-9

 HAL•LEONARD®
CORPORATION

7777 W. BLUEMOUND RD. P.O. BOX 13819 MILWAUKEE, WI 53213

Visit Hal Leonard Online at
www.halleonard.com

AS LONG AS YOU'RE MINE

Music and Lyrics by
STEPHEN SCHWARTZ

FLUTE

With quiet passion

DANCING THROUGH LIFE

FLUTE

Words and Music by
STEPHEN SCHWARTZ

DEFYING GRAVITY

FLUTE

Words and Music by
STEPHEN SCHWARTZ

FOR GOOD

FLUTE

Words and Music by
STEPHEN SCHWARTZ

Tenderly, poco rubato

I COULDN'T BE HAPPIER

FLUTE

Words and Music by
STEPHEN SCHWARTZ

I'M NOT THAT GIRL

FLUTE

Words and Music by
STEPHEN SCHWARTZ

NO GOOD DEED

FLUTE

Words and Music by
STEPHEN SCHWARTZ

Moderato, with intensity
Strings
Play
mf
f
mf
f
p
cresc.
ff

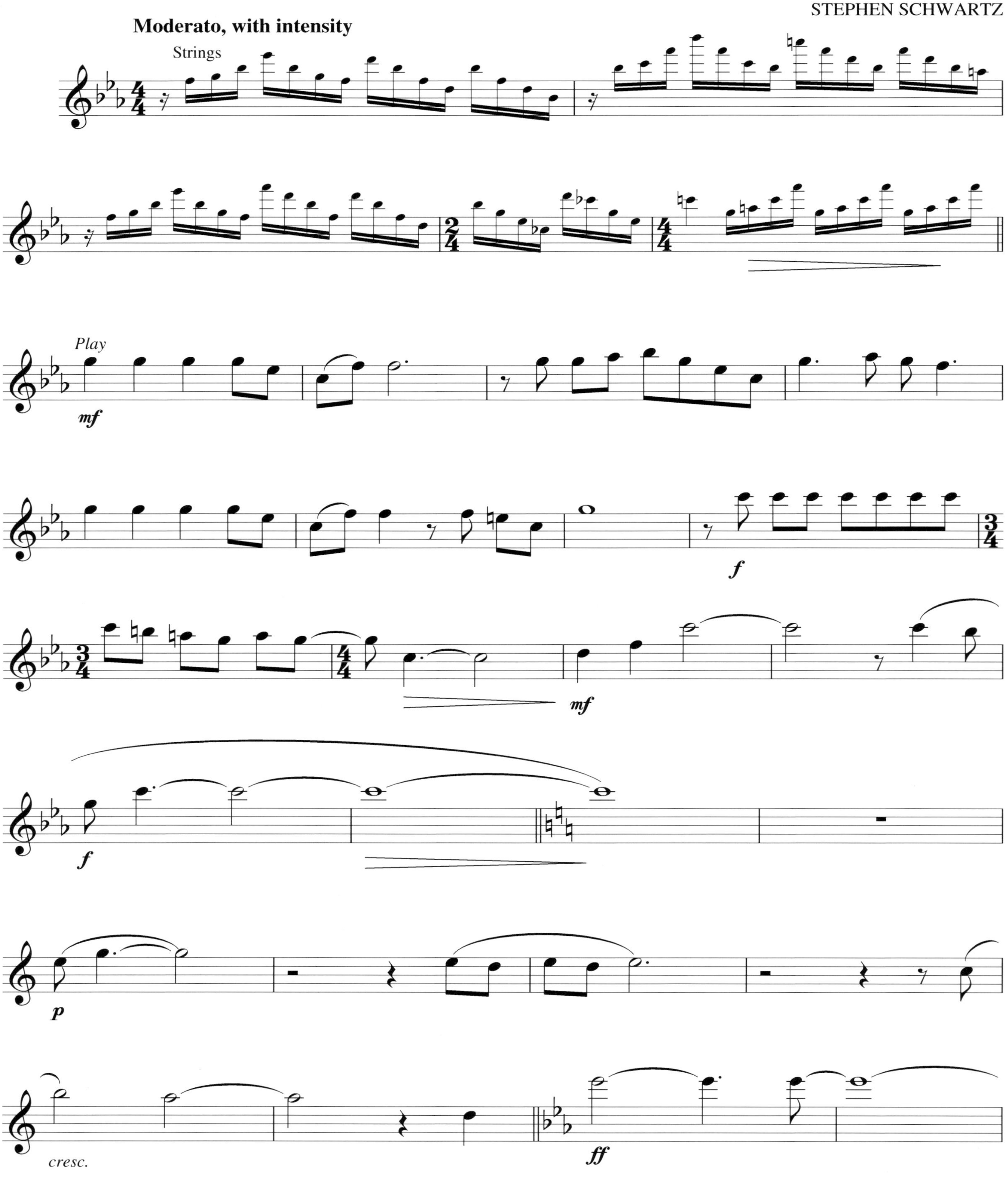

ONE SHORT DAY

FLUTE

Music and Lyrics by
STEPHEN SCHWARTZ

POPULAR

FLUTE

Words and Music by
STEPHEN SCHWARTZ

Sweetly
Music box

molto rit.

Bright and bubbly

cresc.

WHAT IS THIS FEELING?

Words and Music by
STEPHEN SCHWARTZ

FLUTE

THE WIZARD AND I

FLUTE

Words and Music by
STEPHEN SCHWARTZ

WONDERFUL

FLUTE

Music and Lyrics by
STEPHEN SCHWARTZ

NO ONE MOURNS THE WICKED

FLUTE

Words and Music by
STEPHEN SCHWARTZ